巫山小三峡

THE LESSER THREE GORGES OF WUSHAN

解特利 攝影

PHOTO BY：XIE TE LI

中国三峡出版社

CHINA THREE GORGES PUBLISHING HOUSE

小三峽發源地大巴山
小三峽の源——大巴山
Da Ba Mountain … the source of the Lesser Three Gorges.

霧漫峡江
霧の中の小三峡
Fog over the river gorge.

巍巍三峽是馳名中外的旅游勝地。它西起四川省奉節縣白帝城，東至湖北省宜昌市南津關，全長193公里。雄奇偉岸的瞿塘峽，幽深秀美的巫峽，浪急灘險的西陵峽次第相接，組成一條魅力無窮的藝術畫廊，一座無比璀璨的藝術之宮。

峽區內重巒疊嶂，江水紆曲，古木森森，氣勢磅礡。那巍峨的夔門，神秘的風箱峽，嫵媚的神女峯，燈火輝煌的葛洲壩……熔自然景觀與人文景觀于一爐，銘刻下萬代滄桑，蘊孕着千載風華。异域殊方的萬千游子在江水滔滔的平面上，自會渺小于立地接天的峯巒，禁不住在偉哉、雄哉的感嘆中心蕩神搖，從而引發出超越時空的美感。

巍巍としている三峡は名の高い観光地である、西は四川省の奉节县の白帝城から、东は湖北省宜昌市の南津关にいたる。全长192キロメートルで、もつとも峻険な表情を見せることで有名な瞿塘峡、奥深く秀丽な巫峡、浅濑が多く流れも急な西陵は次次と连がり、魅力的な芸術の畫廊と宮殿と組み立てた。

三峡の中に山山と连がり、川が流れまがって、古い木は生々として、雄大な霧囲氣が溢れている。巍巍な夔門、神秘的な風箱峡、なまめかしい神女峰，光り輝く葛洲壩……自然の景色と人造景色と完璧に組みたたて，歴代の苦しみと千年の風流を抱いて异國の観光客は流されていく長江の上で、その三峡の偉さと雄大とは思れず感概無量で時代を超える美しさを感じされるだろう。

The magnificient Three Gorges of the Changjiang River are scenic spots of tourism well-known at home and abroad. They begin from Baidi Town of Fengjie County of Sichuan province in the west and extend to Nantsinguan of Yichang City in the east, with a length of 193 kilometres. The steep and imposing Qutang Gorge, the deep and beautiful Wuxia Gorge and the Xiling Gorge with its shoals and rapids, following on one after another, form up an art gallery of boundless charm, a palace of art of unparalleled brilliance.

In the Gorge regions, there are ranges upon ranges of mountains, winding rivers and dense old trees, all with imposing manners. The lofty Kuimen, the mysterious Bellows Gorge, the charming Peak of Goddess, the brillinatly-lit Gezhouba…etc., merge the natural landscape and human activity together and produce a brilliant record of history. Posing on the floating current, tourists from far and wide will naturally feel their own insignificance before these sky-kissing mountains, and amid the sigh of praise, touch off a sense of beauty which surpasses time and space.

瞿塘峽 西起四川省奉節縣白帝城，東至巫山縣大溪鎮，全長8公里。兩岸陡壁摩天，巍峨對峙，峽內江聲雷鳴，驚濤拍岸。船行其中，頓覺"峰與天關接，舟從地窟行"。

瞿塘峽 西は四川省奉節縣の白帝城から東は巫山縣の大溪鎮まで長さわずか8キロメートルで、兩岸の懸崖は天にもとどかんばかりにそそり立ら、長江の波は岩にたちうねりながら奔走している，舟でそこを通ると「峰と天が連がり，舟が洞窟を行く。」

Qutang Gorge   It begins from Baidi Town of Fengjie County in the west and extends to Daxi Town of Wushan County in the east with a length of 8 kilometres. There are sky-kissing steep precipices facing each other on both banks of the river. Within the gorge, torrents roaring and waves terrifying. It seems that your ship is 'threading through a cellar with sky-kissing mountains over-head'

巫　峽　西起四川省巫山縣大寧河口,東至湖北省巴東縣官渡口,全長 45 公里。峽中千峰競秀,雲雨變幻無窮,幽深秀麗,氣象萬千。名聞遐邇的巫山十二峰即屏列其間。

　　巫峽:西は四川省巫山縣の大寧河口から東は湖北巴東官渡口まで、全長 45 キロメートル、その中に峰峰と排列して、雲と雨が変りやすい、奥深く秀麗な所、有名な巫山十二峰がそこにある。

Wuxia Gorge　It begins from the mouth of the Da Ning River in Wushan County and extends to Guan Du Town of Ba Dong County in Hubei province, with a length of 45 kilometres. There are thousands of beautiful peaks and changing clouds and mists there. The gorge is deep and beautiful. The well-known 12 peaks of Wushan mountain all cluster here.

　　神女峰似若人形、高約 7 米、海拔 912 米。她就是神話傳説中的西天王母娘娘的小女兒、神女瑤姬的化身。

　　神女峰　女性によく似て、高さ約 7 メートル海拔 912 メートル、西王母の一番下の娘で、神女瑤姬から變えた女性である

　　Peak of Goddess　It is 912 metres above sea level and about 7 metres high. As legend had it, it is the incarnation of Yao Ji, the little daughter of Empress of Heaven.

西陵峽 西起湖北省秭歸縣香溪口,東至宜昌市南津關,全長66公里。險灘成陣,泡漩翻滾,江水如沸,以灘多水急著稱。岸邊石灰岩地貌發育,形成千奇百怪的景觀。

西陵峽:西は湖北省の秭歸縣の香溪口から東は宜昌縣の南津關まで、長さ66キロメートル、そこは暗礁が林立して,渦を逆卷き、淺瀬が多く、流れも急な所で、兩岸に石灰岩で妙な景色が見せる。

Xiling Gorge   It begins from the mouth of the Xiangxi River at Zigui County of Hubei and extends to Nanjinguan of Yichang City, with a length of 66 kilometres. Torrential waters roared in the channel which is known as full of shoals and rapids.

大江的驕子——中堡島

中堡島位于湖北省宜昌縣三斗坪鎮,這是一個沉睡了數千年,名不見經傳的江心小島。天賜良機于斯人。二十世紀九十年代,中國人選中這里建築一座經天緯地的宏偉巨構,于是地球人的目光一齊聚焦于這彈丸之地。

盡管舉世矚目的三峽工程淹没區涉及 19 個縣(市),移民達 113 萬,但它功在當代,澤被萬世。大壩總庫容 393 億立方米,其中防洪庫容 221.5 億立方米,裝機容量 1768 萬千瓦,年發電量 840 億度,將給華夏子孫帶來巨大的利益。未來沉入壩底的中堡島自然成爲江之驕子,永標史册。

中堡島は湖北省宜昌縣の三斗坪鎮に位置されている、そこは數千年に名も知らない河の中の小島である、二十世紀九十年代,中國人はそこに立派な建物を建てるつもりで,地球の人人の目をそこに集めた。
有名な三峽水利センターは19縣(市)を水没して,移轉する住民は113萬人で,功績は當代にあり,利益は萬世にもある,タムーの貯水量は393億立方メートル、その中に水防貯水量 221.5 億立方メートル、 電所の設備總容量は1768萬KW,年間 電量は840億KWで、中華の子子孫孫に巨大な利益をもたらしてくれる,壩の底に水没した中堡島は長江の誇りで人人は永遠におぼえるだろう

Zhongbaodao is situated at Sandouping Town of Yichang County. It is an islet dormant for several thousand years and never mentioned in history, but favored now by providence. In 90's of 20th century the Chinese have decided to build the huge dam here. People all over the world have focussed their eyes on this tiny little place.

Although the worldwide attractive Sanxia Project will inundate 10 counties (cities) and 1.13 million people will have to emigrate elsewhere, its meritorious service is beneficial to the present generation and posterity. The capacity of the reservoir of this huge dam will be 39,300,000,000 cubic metres, installed capacity 17,680,600 kilowatts and annual generation of electricity 840,000,000 kw/hours. It will bring to the Chinese people tremendous benefits. Zhongbaodao, which will be sunk into the bottom of the huge dam, will become the favorite son of the Changjiang River and will go down in history.

人間仙境小三峽
仙境小三峽
THE LESSER THREE GORGES ⋯ PARADISE ON EARTH

　　大寧河小三峽依偎在長江三峽的懷抱,被稱為峽中之峽,勝境中的勝境,是大自然的又一杰作。它起于巫峽西口,沿大寧河上溯至涂家壩,全長50公里,由龍門、巴霧、滴翠三峽組成。景區內青山回抱,碧水盈盈,流泉飛瀑,猿鳴鳥啼。玲瓏而不失偉岸,嫵媚中顯出純眞,是一座最具自然情韵的"仙峽"。那摩天的陡壁,聳翠的峯巒,清澈晶瑩的碧波,滾銀翻雪的險灘,色彩斑斕的奇石以及幽靜深邃的峽景使萬千游人陶醉,那隨處可見的懸棺、棧道更讓人在怡美悅趣的游興中,引發出凝重與神秘的思緒。
　　幽幽小三峽,不愧為中華明珠,人間絕景。

　　巫山小三峽は長江三峽の懷にあり、峽の中の峽とよばれ、勝境の中の勝境でもある。それは大自然が造ったもう一つの杰作である。
　　小三峽は西から巫峽の西山に源を　し、人寧川に沿って涂家壩までさかのぼり、その長さが40キロメートルで、龍門、巴霧及び滴翠峽三つの所からできている。
　　それは,青山に囲まれ、紺べきの水が滿滿とただよい、泉が流れ、ばく布が飛び、猿も鳴きながら、鳥も啼きます。そしてその姿が細工に立派でありなまめかしく純真が現われる。さらに、その摩大の斷がい絶壁や、すい綠の峰らんや、澄み切っている紺べきの波や、白波がさかまいている速瀨や、五色の美しい奇石及びもの靜かに奥深い峽景は、大勢の觀光者に陶醉させ、特にあの千年前の崖にあった岩棺と棧道の遺蹟はもっと皆さんに喜んでいる行樂气氛中で深く神秘の考えをそそらせるわけです。
　　幽幽とした小三峽は中華の明珠と世の中の絶景である。

　　The Lesser Three Gorges of the Da Ning River snuggled up to the Three Gorges of the Changjiang River and are known as the gorges in the gorges, the famous scenic spot of the famous scenic spots, another masterpiece of nature. It begins from the west mouth of Wuxia Gorge and extends upstream along the Da Ning River to Tujiaba with a length of 50 kilometres, consisting of the three gorges of Longmen, Bawu and Dicui. In the gorge region, there are sweeping and winding mountains, limpid currents, springs and waterfalls, with monkeys screeching and birds singing. Though exquisite yet high and sturdy; though charming yet pure. It is a 'celestial gorge' of the most romantic natural beauty. The sky-kissing steep precipices, the green peaks, the limpid currents, the roaring rapids, the remarkable colourful stones and the deeply secluded gorge scenery, all attract thousands and thousands of tourists. Hanging coffins and plank roads, which can be seen everywhere, will touch off a deep thinking from the tourists while they enjoy the beautiful scenery.

　　The deep Lesser Three Gorges are really the Pearl of China, the remarkable scenery on earth.

古城巫山
古城巫山
The ancient city of Wushan

寧河入江涇渭明
長江に流れ込んでいる大寧河の水
の色は非常に澄んでいる
Waters of the Da Ning River and that
of the Changjiang River are entirely
different.

巫山烟雲
巫山の霧雲
The mists and clouds of Wushan

巫山旅游碼頭
巫山縣の觀光專用港
Wharf for tourists at Wushan

龍門峽　龍門口至銀窩灘，全長3公里。峽內高壁夾溪，雄冠夔門。

龍門峽　龍門口から銀窩灘まで、全長3キロメートルで，絶壁の門に流れがれ，夔門に負けないような雄大さがある

Longmen Gorge　It is from Longmenkou to Yinwotan with a length of 3 kilometres. There are high precipices and narrow streams, more magnificent than Kuimen.

柳葉舟
柳葉舟と言う舟
Willow-leaf boat

龍門峽
龍門峽
Longmen Gorge

15

16

龍門碼頭
龍門港
Wharf at Longmen

龍門橋是一道橫跨龍門峽口兩岸絶壁上的大橋。橋長 180 米, 寬 11 米, 跨度 122 米, 離河面 102 米。1987 年 10 月竣工通車。

龍門橋:龍門峽の入口にある大橋で, 長さ180メートル, 高さ102メートルで, 1987 年 10 月オープンしたもの

Longmen Bridge It is a big bridge spanning the steep precipices on both banks at the mouth of Longmen Gorge. It is 180 metres long, 11 metre wide, with a span of 122 metres and 102 metres above the river. It was built and opened to traffic in October, 1987.

龍門大橋
龍門大橋
The Longmen Bridge

龍門泉
龍門の泉
The Longmen Spring

銀窩灘
銀窩灘
Yinwotan shoal

九龍柱靈芝峰
九龍柱と靈芝峰
Peak of Magic Fungus of
the Nine Dragon Column

古棧道遺迹
古棧道の遺址
Ruins of ancient plank road

　　古棧道。小三峽西岸絶壁上，有一排列整齊的小石孔。孔距 1.7 米、孔深 0.7 米、見方 0.02 米、一直延伸到陜西省境内。長約 300 余公里，這就是我國最長的一條古棧道遺迹。

　　古棧道：小三峽の西岸の絶壁の上にきらんと排列している小さい石の穴がある，穴と穴との距離は5尺で，深さ2尺，タテとヨコともに6寸で，長さ300キロメートル，陜西省まで續けている、これは中國では最も長い古棧道である。

　　The ancient plank road　　In the steep precipice on the west bank of the Lesser Three Gorges, there is a range of orderly small holes. The distance between them is 5 ft.. The hole is 2 ft. deep and 6 inches square. The range extends to Shan Xi province with a length about 300 Kilometres. It is the ruins of the longest ancient plank road in China.

琵琶洲
琵琶洲
Pi Pa Islet

熊貓洞
パンタの顔によく似でる洞窟
Cave of the panda

寧河晨曦
寧河の早
Dawn over the Da Ning River

放灘
瀬の上に流れる舟
Sailing down the shoal

雨後峡江水由緑變黄
雨の後、川の水は緑から黄くになった
The green river gorge became yellow after rain

巴霧峽　東坪壩至太平灘,全長約 10 公里,峽内崖高壑深,雲蒸霧涌,怪石狀物,似幻若真。

　　巴霧峽　東坪壩から太平灘まで、長さ10キロメートル、そこは崖壁高い、雲霧があふれて造型奇抜な鍾乳石が一派ある

Bawu Gorge　It is from Dongpingba to Taipingtan, With a length about 10 kilometres. There are high cliffs and deep valleys, lingering clouds and mists and variegated and fanciful stones.

巴霧峽
巴霧峽
Bawu Gorge

水似青蘿帶
水は青帯のように
The water flows like a green ribbon

龍進
龍進
Dragon going in

虎出
虎出
Tiger coming out

馬歸山
馬歸山
Ma Gui Hill

水上流星
飛ぶように過ぎ去った舟
The flying boat

蓮臺峰
蓮臺の峰
Peak of Lotus Throne

猴子撈月
猿は水の中の月を取る
The monkey is fishing the moon.

烏龜下蛋
龜の卵
Turtle laying eggs

犁浪
犁の波
Ploughing the waves

巴霧峡懸棺。巴霧峡絶壁上的洞穴里，有一漆黑的棺木，距河面約 500 米，這是古人死后葬身的懸棺。

巴霧峡岩棺：巴霧峡の絶壁の洞窟に黒い棺木がある，川から500メートルの高い所にあり，これは昔の人がなくなったあと，葬する岩棺。

The hanging coffin at Bawu Gorge　In a cave in the steep precipice at Bawu Gorge, there is a black coffin, about 500 metres high above the river. It is the hanging coffin of an ancient person.

巫山博物館陳列的懸棺
巫山博物館に展覧されている岩棺
Hanging coffin exhibited at the Wushan Museum.

飛雲洞懸棺
飛雲洞の岩棺
Hanging coffin in the Flying Cave

巴霧峡懸棺
巴霧峡の岩棺
Hanging coffin in the Bawu Gorge

寧河上游懸棺
寧河上流の岩棺
Hanging coffins at the upper reaches of the Da Ning River

荊竹壩懸棺
荊竹坝の岩棺
Hanging coffin at Jing Zhu ridge

滴翠峽懸棺
滴翠峽の岩棺
Hanging coffin in Dicui Gorge

清澈的大寧河河底的石頭上，長着綠色的苔絲，隨水飄逸，好似姑娘美麗的秀髮。

　苔絲：清い大寧河の底の石の上に、綠の苔蘚植物がある、水にたたよって、若い娘の髮の毛みたいである。

　The bryphite   On the stones at the bottom of the limpid Da Ning River, there grow the green bryophite. They sway and drift with the current, just like a beautiful girl's hair.

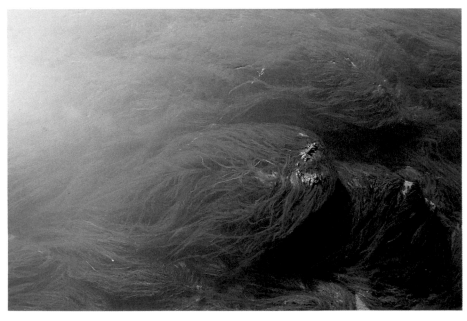

苔絲
系を垂らしたような苔蘚物植
The bryophite

34

光與影
光と影
Light and shadow

小三峽雨花石
小三峽の雨花石
Colourful stones of the Lesser Three Gorges

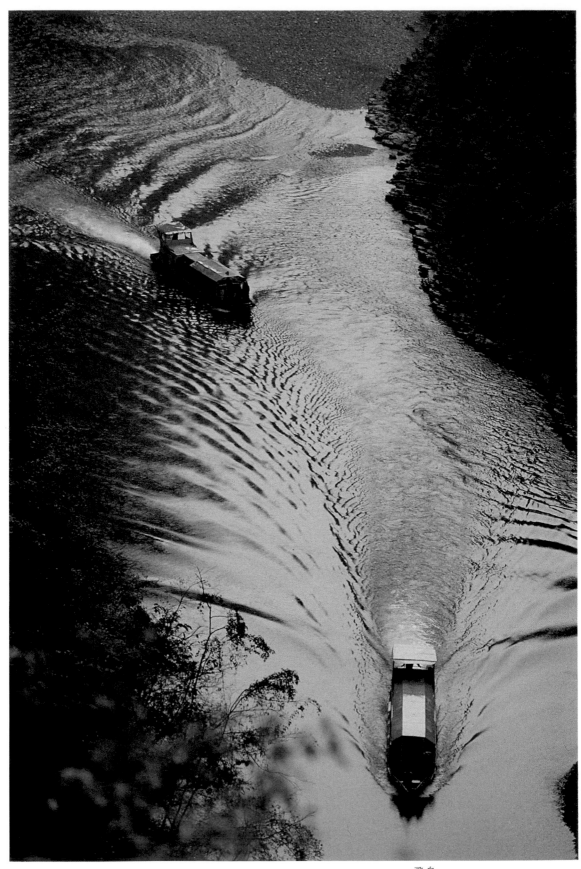

飛舟
飛ぶように過ぎ去った舟
The flying boat

雙龍索橋
双龍鎮の吊橋
The Shuang Long Cable bridge

雙龍鎮
双龍鎮
Shuang Long Town

輕舟已過萬重山
輕舟すでにすぐ万重の山
The skiff had left behind it ten thousand ranges of hills.

彎彎大寧河
曲がりくれった大寧河
The winding Da Ning River

滴翠峽 雙龍鎮至涂家壩, 全長約 20 公里, 峽内銀泉凌空, 峰巒叠翠, 山青水碧, 古藤搖曳。

3. 滴翠峽　双龍鎮から涂家壩まで, 全長 20 キロメートル
そこに青青とした峰峰か連がり山紫水明な絶景があり, 古い木木がしなやかに風に揺れている。

Dicui Gorge　It is from Shuang Long Town to Tugiaba, with a length of 20 kilometres. There are flying springs, green peaks, limpid streams and old swaying rattans there.

棧道・索橋
棧道・吊橋
Cable bridge on the plank road

秋意
秋
Feelings of autumn

天在峰外缺處明
天在峰外缺處明
The sky gleams through the gap between the peaks

滴翠峡
滴翠峡
Dicui Gorge

競發
舟の仕合
Boat-racing

彩峽
色とりとりの峽谷
Colourful Gorge

43

羅家寨距河面 80 余米，寨基 400 平方米，石砌寨牆，附岩危立。是古人羅秀才攻書的地方。

羅家寨：川から80メートル高い所に面積 400 平方メートル，石の壁で岩によって立っている，ここは昔の羅秀才が勉強した所だ。

Luo Gia Stockade It is about 80 metres above the river, with a foundation of 400 squre metres. Its walls were built with stones, laid on the brink of the precipice. It is the place where Luo, the Xiucai (scholar) had studied there.

羅家寨
羅家寨
Luo Gia Stockade

天泉飛雨
天泉飛雨
Drizzling of the Heavenly Spring

水簾洞
水簾洞
Cave of water screen

滴
滴り
Dropping

綿羊崖
綿羊崖
The Sheep Crag

猴
猿
Monkeys

小三峡娃娃魚
小三峡のサンショウウオ
Salamander of the Lesser Three Gorges

野鴛鴦
野生の鴛鴦
The wild mandarin ducks

别有洞天
别天地
Place of enchanting beauty

秋游
秋の旅
Autumn excursion

雙鷹戲屏
双鹰戏屏
Eagles playing on the screen

摩岩佛像
摩岩佛像
Buddhas carved out of the cliffs

馬渡河小賣市場
馬渡河の露天市場
Peddlery market at the Ma Du River

小三峡秋色
小三峡の秋
Autumn at the Lesser Three Gorges

兩岸青山相對出
兩岸の青山
Green mountains facing each other on both banks of the
river

畫中游
絵の旅
Touring in a pictureque scene

霜葉紅似二月花
春の花のように赤々と
している紅葉
The frosty leaves as red as
the flowers of early
spring.

旅游新景——小小三峡
新しい觀光地——小小三峡
NEW SCENERY OF TOURISM ⋯ THE LESSER OF THE LESSER THREE GORGES

　　小小三峡位于大寧河支流馬渡河內,是名播宇內的小三峡的子峡,全程15公里。由三撑峡、秦王峡、長灘峡組成。峡內充滿原始的野趣,蕨葉覆道,古藤挂空,溶洞深深,長灘幽幽。行游其中,定能感受到超凡脫俗、歸眞返樸之樂。此景區1992年始開發,游人摩肩接踵,競相前往,以爭睹她誘人的風采。

　　小小三峡な大寧河の支流の馬渡河にあり、名の高い小三峡の「子峡」である、長さ15キロメートルで,三撑峡,秦王峡と長灘峡三つの所からできている,その中に原始的なわもしろさ、しだ植物と古い木木がどこでも見える。深い鍾乳洞と長い瀬など、觀光客はきっと大自然に涙るようなおもしろさを感じるだろう、ここは1992年から開放されて、多くの人人はそこへ行ってすばらしい風采を觀學します

　　The Lesser of the Lesser Three Gorges are situated in the Madu River, a tributary river of the Da Ning River which is a well-known sub-gorge of the Lesser Three Gorges. Its length is 15 kilometres and consists of Sanchang Gorge, Qinwang Gorge and Changtan Gorge. There is interesting primitive wildness in these gorges. Brakes cover the roads and old rattans hang overhead, karst caves deep and shoals long. Sauntering in them you would feel happily that you have held yourself aloof from the worldly affairs and returned to original simplicity. This scenic spot was first opened and developed in 1992. Tourists have thronged to go there to see the beauty there.

飄
飘う
Drifting

小小三峡
小小三峡
The Lesser of the Lesser Three Gorges

纖夫
船を曳く勞動者
Trackers

仙乳石
鍾乳石
The stone of Magic Milk

馬渡河小小三峡峡口
馬渡河小小三峡の入口
The mouth of the Lesser of the Lesser Three Gorges on
the Ma Du River

世外桃園
世外桃园
The Land of Peach Blossoms (haven of peace)

多姿多彩的民俗風情
多彩な民間風俗
THE VARIEGATED LOCAL CUSTOMS AND CONDITIONS

　　大江東去,歲月如斯。大溪文化透露出人類文明的曙光,而后通過大江、大峽、大山、大谷的陶冶,通過巴蜀文化與荊楚文化的交融,于是久遠的歷史用鋒利的刻刀鑄出獨具風韵的三峽文化,釀就具有濃鬱地方色彩的民俗風情。那粗獷驃悍的巴山漢子,那勤勞勇健的三峽女兒,用甜甜的峽聲、峽語道出憨厚與樸實,用巴渝舞、竹枝歌展示出美的律動。白包帕、旱烟袋里裝着智慧的思考,丁字杵、扁背兜里馱着生活的希翼,而那聲聲嗩吶、陣陣鑼鼓正在頑強地迎接生命的延續……

吊腳樓
吊腳樓
Storied house with supporting poles

大河は東に流れていき，岁月は早いもので，大溪文化は人類の文明の兆が射していきた、大江、大峽、大山、大谷の陶やすることで巴蜀文化と荊楚文化が産み出きた，温厚な民間風俗がある、荒削りな男、勤勉でそぼくな女性、甘い"峽聲、峽語"で言った、まじめさとそぼくさ，巴渝舞と竹枝歌で美しさを表わす、白いタオルとはタバコの中に智慧の考えがあり，「丁」と言う型をした勞働道具に生活の望みが含んでいる、チャルメラと太鼓の演奏の中で強く生命の續きを迎える。

The Changjiang River flows eastward incessantly and time goes by. The Daxi Culture reveals the dawn of human civilization and then, through the moulding of rivers, gorges, mountains and valleys, through the blending of Bashu Culture and the Jingchu Culture, the distant history carved out the Sanxia Culture with a sharp knife, and produced the rich colourful local customs and conditions.

The bold and agile man of Ba Shan, the diligent and brave girls of Sanxia speak out their simplicity and good nature with the sweet Sanxia language and the Bayu dances and the Zhu-Zhi-Chi-folk songs reveal the charm of a rhythmic beauty. The white turbans and tobacco pouches contain wisdom and thinking, the T pestles and bamboo baskets on the back carry the hope of life, while the horns and gongs and drums are vehemently meeting the continuity of life.……

老街黄桷樹
町の木
The bunyan tree at Laojie

甜妹.
樂しい娘
Girl of sweet

祖母
お祖母さん
The grandma

淘豬草
ぶた飼を洗う
Gathering grass for the pigs

幺嫂
おばさん
The youngest sister-in-law

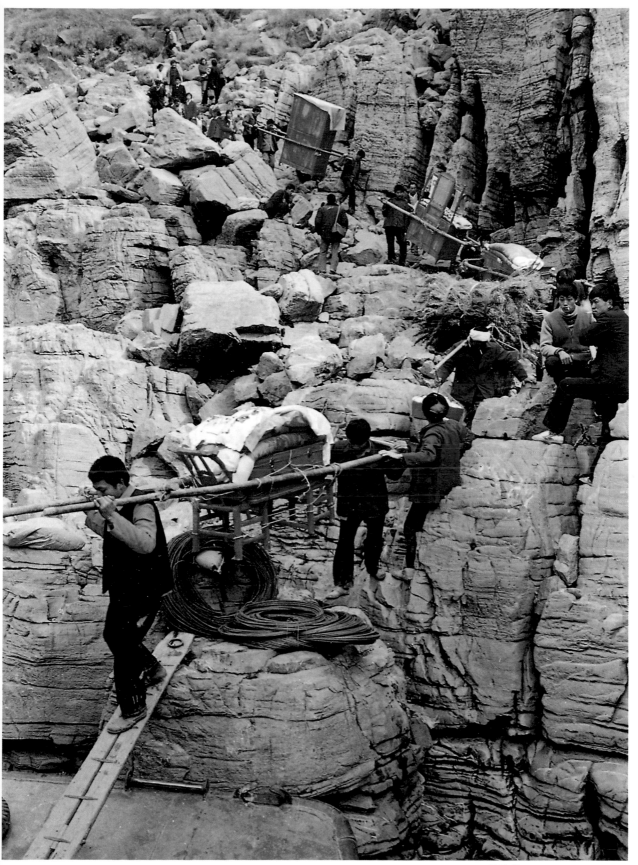

送嫁妆
嫁入り道具を送る
Delivering the dowry

61

山路彎彎
曲がりくねった山道
The winding mountain path

放牛娃
牛飼い子供
The cowboy

船工的午餐
船頭たちの昼飯
Lunch of the boatman

夏收的日子
夏の収穫の日日
Harvest season in summer

稱肥豬
豚を量る
Weighing the fat pig

很甜很甜的
甘いのよ
Pleasantly sweet

大昌古鎮是一座有着 1700 年歷史的古鎮、鎮内現存建築多爲明末清初所建, 距今已 300 多年。

大昌古鎮：1700 年の歴史がある古い町で, いま保存している建物は明の末と清の始めごろの物, いままで300 年ぐらいの歴史がある。

The ancient town of Dachang
It is an ancient town with a history more than 1,700 years. Most of the buildings there were built at the end of the Ming Dynasty and the beginning of the Qing Dynasty over 300 years ago.

老姐妹相逢
巡り合う姉妹
Meeting of two old sisters

夕陽
夕燒け
The sunset

索橋
吊橋
Cable bridge.

峡江飛瀑
小三峡の瀑布
The flying waterfall on the river in the gorge

67

曙光
寧河の早
Dawn over the Da Ning River

69

巫山小三峽示意圖 THE LESSER THREE GORGES OF WUSHAN

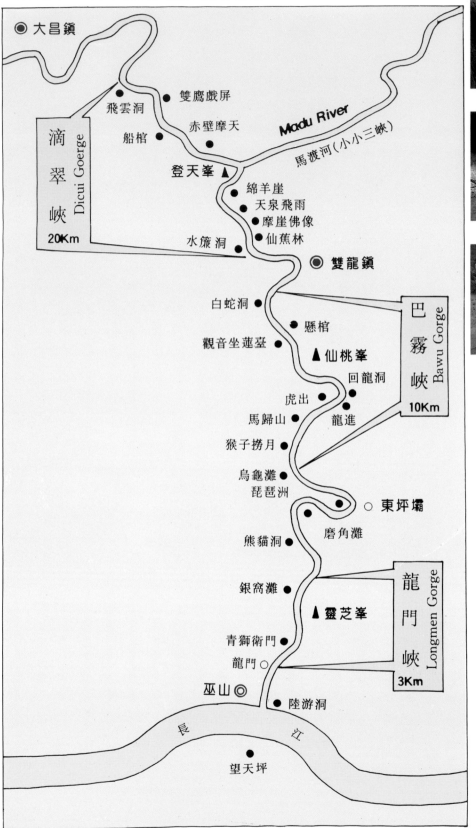

◎ 大昌鎮

Madu River

馬渡河(小小三峽)

飛雲洞
船棺
雙鷹戲屏
赤壁摩天

滴翠峽 Dicui Goerge
20Km

登天峯 ▲

綿羊崖
天泉飛雨
摩崖佛像
水簾洞
仙蕉林

◎ 雙龍鎮

白蛇洞
懸棺
觀音坐蓮臺
▲ 仙桃峯

回龍洞
虎出
馬歸山
龍進
猴子撈月
烏龜灘
琵琶洲

巴霧峽 Bawu Gorge
10Km

○ 東坪壩

熊貓洞
磨角灘
銀窩灘
▲ 靈芝峯
青獅銜門
龍門 ○

龍門峽 Longmen Gorge
3Km

巫山 ◎
陸游洞

長江

望天坪

作者简介

解特利,中国摄影家协会会员,中国艺术摄影学会会员,重庆市摄影家协会理事,副研究馆员,现在重庆市巫山县文化馆工作。

从 1980 年开始对长江三峡进行系统的摄影创作工作,近 20 年来,长期跋涉于三峡之中,拍摄了大量的有关长江三峡和三峡库区淹没城镇的珍贵资料以及优美的三峡风光照片。曾先后应邀到上海、重庆、无锡、广州、深圳、珠海等城市举办《三峡风情》个人摄影艺术展览。其三峡摄影作品还多次在国内外展出,获奖和被收藏。出版有《长江三峡》、《巫山小三峡》个人摄影画册。本人艺术传略载入《中国摄影家大辞典》、《中国当代艺术界名人录》。

解特利は中国摄影家協会の会員、中国芸術摄影学会の会員,重慶市摄影家協会の理事,副研究館員である。現在,重慶市巫山県文化館に勤め。

1980 年から,長江三峡のシリーズ摄影創作が始め,20 年あまりの長い間三峡地区を見てまわり,大量の長江三峡に関する写真と三峡ダム地区水没される町の珍しい資料及びきれいな三峡景色の写真を摄った。上海、重慶、無錫、広州、深圳、珠海などの町で「三峡風情」という個人摄影芸術展示会が行われた。その中の三峡摄影作品が何回も国内外で展示され,受賞され,収蔵された。出版された個人写真集は「長江三峡」、「巫山小三峡」など。本人の芸術伝が《中国摄影大辞典》,《中国当代芸術界名人録》に収められている。

Xie Te Li, Member of the Chinese Photographers Association, member of the Chinese Artistic Photography Society, standing member of executive of the Chongqing City Photographers Association, assistant reseracher, is now working in the Culture Center of Wushan County of Chongqing City.

Beginning from 1980, he started systematic creative photographing of the Three Gorges of the Changjiang River. For the last 20 years, he has traversed in the Three Gorges, taking lots of precious photos of the Three Gorges and the inundated cities and towns as well as those of the scenery in the gorges. He has been invited to Shanghai, Chongqing, Wuxi, Guangzhou, Shen Zhen and Zhu Hai to put on personal exhibitions of artistic photos of "The Bearing of the Three Gorges". His photos of the Three Gorges had been on exhibition at home and abroad and won prizes and collected by photo fans. Published are his photo albums "The Three Gorges of the Changjiang River", "The Minor Three Gorges of Wushan". His brief artistic biography is included in "The Dictionary of Chinese Photographers" and "Who's Who of contemporary Chinese artistic world".

圖書在版編目(CIP)數據

巫山小三峽/解特利主編 . − 北京:中國三峽出版社,
1997.3
ISBN 7 − 80099 − 260 − 8

Ⅰ.巫… Ⅱ.解… Ⅲ.風光攝影-攝影集-中國-現代 Ⅳ
.J426

中國版本圖書館 CIP 數據核字(97)第 03428 號

主　　編:解特利
責任編輯:呂福元
　　　　　喬德炳(特邀)
撰　　文:胡亞星
英文翻譯:曾均甫
日文翻譯:李　雲
裝幀設計:喬德炳

Executive editors: Lu Fu Yuan, Qiao De Bing.
Articles: Hu Zheng Xing.
Translator of English: Zeng Jun Fu.
Translator of Japanese: Li Yun.
Design: Qiao De Bing.

巫山小三峽　　解特利　主編

中國三峽出版社
(北京市海澱區蔡公莊一號)
四川省印刷制版中心 印制
開本:787×1092 毫米 1/16 印張:4.5
1997 年 3 月第 1 版　1997 年 3 月第 1 次印刷
印數:1—3000 冊

ISBN 7 − 80099 − 260 − 8/J·53